# Science Around You

# Bugs in the Garden

## Susan Martineau

### illustrated by Leighton Noyes

with thanks to Kathryn Higgins,
Head of Chemistry, Leighton Park School

# contents

# How to be a Scientist

Scientists learn about the world around us by doing experiments. You will learn about the science in your garden or park in this book. You won't need any special equipment for these experiments. They use everyday things you'll probably find at home already. Don't forget to ask a grown-up before using them. Before you begin, always read through the whole experiment to make sure you have everything you need.

**BE SAFE!**
Ask a grown-up before you go out into the garden and never go to the park on your own.

Keep a notebook handy so you can draw or write up what happens like a real scientist. You can make up your own experiments too.

**Words to Know** Special science words are explained on page 24.

Wash your hands when you've finished outside.

Never eat anything you find in the garden or park. Some plants and berries can be very bad for you.

**Quick Quizzer** answers are on p.24.

3

# Bug Hunt

See what mini-beasts you can find living in your garden or in the park. The best time to look for them is in warm weather when creepy crawlies are the most active. You might want to wear gloves when you are poking about looking for bugs!

**1.** Take a notebook, magnifying glass and pencil out into the garden or the park.

Spider

**2.** Choose a small area of flowerbed or lawn. Look in the soil, under stones and in long grass.

Butterfly

**3.** When you find a bug, draw it in your notebook. Count the legs, wings and parts of its body. Is it wriggling or crawling?

Worm

Snail

Caterpillar

Centipede

Beetle

Slug

Ant

4

Beetle

## Quick Quizzer!
What has eight legs and spins a web?

Centipede

Spider

Snail

Butterfly

## Let's Take a Closer Look!

The proper name for creepy crawlies is INVERTEBRATES. This word means an animal without a backbone. Not all INVERTEBRATES are INSECTS though. INSECTS have six legs and three parts to their bodies. So an ant is an INSECT but worms, snails and spiders are not.

Caterpillar

## Try This!

If you don't know the name of the bugs you've found you can ask a grown-up or look it up in books about mini-beasts. You can find out lots of fascinating facts about these creatures.

Worm

## Quick Warning!

Take a grown-up with you on a bug hunt. (They can carry a drink or a snack for you!) Don't pick the bugs up in case they could sting or hurt you. You don't want to risk hurting them either.

Ant

Slug

5

# Worm Home

You'll need three or four earthworms for this experiment. Look for them in freshly dug soil or under stones and logs. Pick them up very carefully so you don't hurt them. Leave the Worm Home in a cool, dark place for a few days and watch what the worms do.

**1.** Ask a grown-up to help cut the top off a plastic bottle.

**2.** Put layers of soil and sand in the bottle. Sprinkle with water.

**3.** Place some leaves and grass on top. Gently add your worms.

**4.** Tape some dark paper around the bottle. Put it in a cool, dark place.

# Let's Take a Closer Look!

The earthworms make tunnels through the soil and sand layers. In the garden these tunnels help air and water to reach the roots of plants. Worms also pull leaves down into the soil and this makes NUTRIENTS, or food, for plants. Worms help the plants to grow well.

## Worm Warning!
Set your worms free after a few days!

## Quick Quizzer!
Which garden creature loves to eat worms?

Clue: there's one on this page.

Worm casts are curly piles of soil left behind by worms. It's worm poo.

## Did You Know?
The largest earthworms in the world live in Australia, South Africa and South America. They can be up to 3 metres long!

# Sprouting Beans

Growing things is good fun and very easy. Beans, seeds and nuts are the parts of plants and trees that grow into new plants and trees. It takes a few days to sprout these beans so be patient! To cover the jar, use a piece of clean, disposable washing-up cloth.

**1.** Put a small handful of mung beans in a bowl of cold water for the night.

**2.** Rinse and drain in a sieve. Put the beans into an old jam jar.

**3.** Cover the jar with a piece of clean washing-up cloth. Secure with an elastic band. Leave jar in a warm place.

**4.** Uncover the jar and rinse the beans twice a day. Put the cloth back on and drain the beans through it.

## Did You Know?

Beans, seeds and nuts are spread around your garden in all sorts of ways so that they can grow into new plants and trees. Some are carried off by the wind. Some seeds inside fruit and berries are spread when birds eat them and then leave them behind in their droppings.

## Quick Fact

Coconuts are the seeds of palm trees. Their shells are waterproof so they can float and be carried by the sea.

Lie the jar on its side so the beans can spread out.

## Let's Take a closer Look!

The beans swell up after their night in cold water. On the second day in the jar small white sprouts grow out of the beans. This is called GERMINATION. When these sprouts are about 1-2 cm long you can rinse and eat them. The beans need light, water and warmth to grow well.

9

# Plant Power

Plants and trees need water to grow.
They take water in through their roots in the ground.
This experiment shows you how the water moves
around plants and trees. Use any food colouring
you like for this experiment but red is really good.

**1.** Mix some food colouring with water in an old jam jar or beaker.

**2.** Put a stick of celery, with its leaves still on, into the water.

**3.** Watch and note what happens to the colour of the celery over the next two days.

# Did You Know?

Plants that grow in very dry places, like deserts, have to be good at storing water. They have large, juicy stems and leaves. Cacti are plants that can live in places without much rain.

Ouch, don't sit on that plant!

## Let's Take a Closer Look!

Red marks start to appear on the celery leaves after a few hours. Over the next two days more and more red appears on the leaves. Water carries food to all parts of a plant or tree. This experiment shows you how water travels from the roots of a plant all the way up to its leaves.

## Quick Fact!

Some trees in the rainforest can grow as tall as a twenty-storey building. Think of all the water going round inside them!

# Cloud Code

You will need your notebook for this experiment. You are going to keep a cloud diary to see how the different shapes of clouds tell us about the weather and what it will do next. It's like a kind of code in the sky.

**1.** Go out each day with your notebook and a pencil. Look up into the sky.

**2.** Draw or write down what the clouds look like. What is their shape, colour and size?

**3.** Make a note of what the weather is like each day and if it changes as the clouds change.

It's freezing cold today.

So the clouds aren't made of cottonwool then?

# Let's Take a Closer Look!

Clouds are made of tiny water drops or ice crystals. CUMULUS clouds are big and fluffy. White ones mean good weather, dark ones (called CUMULONIMBUS) bring heavy rain. STRATUS clouds are low, pale-grey clouds covering the sky. They often bring light rain. CIRRUS clouds are streaky, wispy and high in the sky. They mean windy weather and maybe storms to come.

## Try This!

Ask a grown-up if there is a THERMOMETER you can use out in the garden or park. A THERMOMETER tells you how warm or cold it is. You can write this in your notebook too.

## Quick Fact

Scientists who study the weather are called METEOROLOGISTS. They give us weather forecasts to tell us what the weather will do next.

# Rain Catcher

Make a simple gadget to catch and measure how much rain falls. You'll need an old jar or clear plastic beaker with straight sides, a small funnel and a ruler. Use some blobs of sticky tack to fix the funnel in place and stop the wind blowing it away.

**1.** Put the funnel into the top of the jar or beaker. Place the Rain Catcher outside in an open space.

**2.** Check it each day at the same time. Use the ruler to measure how many centimetres of rain have fallen.

**3.** Empty the jar each time and put it back in the same place.

**4.** Note the amount of rain each time in your notebook.

## Quick Quizzer!

Can you remember the name given to big, fluffy rain clouds?

Clue: look back at page 13.

## Did You Know?

It's really important to know what the weather is going to be like for lots of people. For example, farmers need to know when it will rain to decide when to plant their crops and to make sure they will grow properly.

Don't waste the water in the Catcher. Water the plants!

## Let's Take a Closer Look!

Rain falls when the tiny water drops in clouds join up to make bigger ones. They get so big and heavy that they fall to the ground. The Sun heats up water on the ground and turns it into WATER VAPOUR. This rises into the air. As the WATER VAPOUR goes higher it starts to cool down and turns back into water drops. These make more clouds and it rains again!

15

# Growing Shadows

If you go outside on a sunny day you will see that you have a shadow. This is because your body is blocking the light of the Sun. It can't get through you to reach the ground. This experiment will show you what happens to your shadow at different times of the day.

**1.** Take a friend, your notebook and a tape measure out into the park or the garden on a sunny morning.

**2.** Take it in turns to stand still and measure each other's shadows.

**3.** Do the same thing in the middle of the day and again in the late afternoon.

**4.** Write down the measurements in your notebook each time.

## Quick Fact

Before there were clocks, shadows were used to tell the time with something called a sundial.

Moon    Earth

Sun

Moon's shadow on Earth

## Did You Know?

A special shadow called a SOLAR ECLIPSE happens when the Moon moves between the Earth and the Sun. The Moon blocks the light of the Sun and the Moon's shadow falls on a part of the Earth.

## Let's Take a Closer Look!

When the Sun is low in the sky in the morning and evening your body blocks out more of its light and so your shadow is long. At midday the Sun is high in the sky and your body blocks out less of its light. This makes your shadow shorter.

# Rainbow Magic

Did you know that light is really a mixture of different colours? In this experiment you are going to make these different colours appear. Ask a grown-up first before using the hosepipe in the garden. If you haven't got one then perhaps you can find a friend who has.

**1.** Go out into the garden on a sunny day.

**2.** Point the hosepipe away from you towards a dark fence or wall.

**3.** Stand with your back to the Sun and turn the water on.

**4.** See what colours you can spot in the spray.

## Did You Know?

When it is raining and the Sun is shining at the same time you might be able to spot a rainbow. The colours of a rainbow always appear in the same order: red, orange, yellow, green, blue, indigo and violet.

Don't spray me. I don't like getting wet!

## Let's Take a Closer Look!

Light looks white but really it is made of many colours. When the Sun shines through the water spray, the water splits the light into all these colours, and we see a rainbow. If you could mix them back together again this would make white light.

# Gravity Jump

Have you ever wondered why you don't just float off into the air when you go outside? In this experiment you are going to find out about the special force that keeps us all on the ground.

**1.** Go out into the garden or to the park.

**2.** Take some friends, and a grown-up, with you.

**3.** Ask your friends to jump the highest they can into the air.

**4.** Maybe ask the grown-up too!

# Let's Take a Closer Look!

When you jump into the air all the muscles in your body have to work hard to push you up. They have to work hard because there is an invisible force called GRAVITY that is pulling you towards the ground. The stronger your muscles are, the higher you will be able to jump but you will always come back to Earth!

## Did You Know?

To get into space, a rocket needs very powerful engines to push against the Earth's gravity. It needs to go about ten times faster than a bullet! In space, away from the Earth's gravity, astronauts have to have their food and drink in special packs to stop it all floating away.

## Quick Fact

It is gravity that makes things fall down to the ground when we drop them.

# The Sky at Night

You are going to be an astronomer in this experiment. Astronomers are scientists who study the stars. Choose a clear night when the sky is not cloudy. Go out into the dark and look up into the night sky. You will see more if you can get away from street and house lights. Make sure you take a grown-up with you.

**1.** Take a notebook, pencil and a small torch into the garden or park.

**2.** Find somewhere to sit down and look up into the sky.

**3.** Write down and draw what you see. If you see patterns in the stars, then draw them.

The Plough

The Southern Cross

# Did You Know?

Different patterns of stars have been given names by ASTRONOMERS. The patterns are called CONSTELLATIONS. You might be able to spot The Plough (or Big Dipper) if you live in the Northern half of the world. In the Southern half, look out for the Southern Cross.

Don't mistake an aeroplane for a star. Aeroplanes have green and red lights on them.

## Quick Quizzer

What do we call the force that keeps the Moon going around the Earth instead of just floating off?

Clue: it stops us from floating off the Earth too.

## Let's Take a Closer Look!

The Moon is big and easy to spot. It ORBITS, or goes round, our Earth once every 28 days and you will see different parts of it as it moves round. On a clear night you will also see thousands of stars twinkling in the sky. Stars are huge balls of very hot gases sending out heat and light.

# Words to Know

**Astronomer** – Scientist who studies the stars and everything in space.

**Cirrus** – These are high, wispy clouds.

**Constellations** – These are patterns of stars in the sky. Astronomers give them names.

**Cumulus** – These are big, fluffy clouds.

**Cumulonimbus** – These are big, storm clouds.

**Germination** – This is when a seed, nut or bean first starts to grow.

**Gravity** – A force that pulls things towards the Earth.

**Insect** – An invertebrate with six legs and three parts to its body.

**Invertebrate** – A creature without a backbone.

**Meteorologist** – Scientist who studies the weather.

**Nutrients** – The foodstuff that plants or animals need to grow well. Plants get nutrients from the soil.

**Orbit** – The path of something that is travelling around a star or planet. The Earth orbits the Sun. The Moon orbits the Earth.

**Solar Eclipse** – This is when the Moon moves between the Earth and the Sun and the Moon's shadow falls on part of the Earth.

**Stratus** – These are low sheets of clouds, covering the sky.

**Thermometer** – This is a gadget that tells you how hot or cold the air is.

**Water Vapour** – The invisible gas that is made when the Sun heats up water. It is also made when a kettle boils water.

## Quizzer Answers

Page 5 – a spider
Page 7 – a bird
Page 15 – Cumulonimbus
Page 19 – seven
Page 23 – gravity